FRUITA 8-9 LIF

MW00578397

STATES

TEXAS

A MyReportLinks.com Book

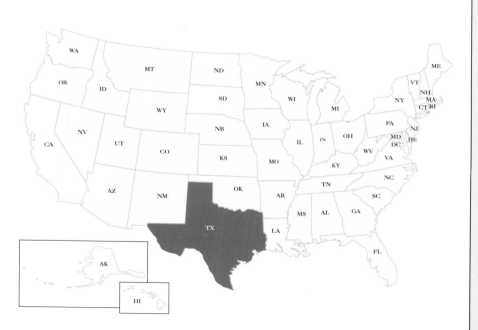

Judy Alter

MyReportLinks.com Books

an imprint of

Enslow Publishers, Inc. E

Box 398, 40 Industrial Road
Berkeley Heights, NJ 07922
USA

MyReportLinks.com Books, an imprint of Enslow Publishers, Inc. MyReportLinks®
is a registered trademark of Enslow Publishers, Inc.

Copyright © 2002 by Enslow Publishers, Inc.

All rights reserved.

No part of this book may be reproduced by any means
without the written permission of the publisher.

Library of Congress Cataloging-in-Publication Data

Alter, Judy, 1938–
    Texas / Judy Alter.
        p. cm. — (States)
    Includes bibliographical references and index.
    Summary: Discusses the land and climate, economy, government, and
history of the state of Texas.
    ISBN 0-7660-5018-1
    1. Texas—Juvenile literature. [1. Texas.] I. Title. II. Series:
States (Series : Berkeley Heights, N.J.)
F386.3.A648 2002
976.4—dc21
                                                                2001004314

                        2006

Printed in the United States of America

10 9 8 7 6 5 4 3 2

To Our Readers:
Through the purchase of this book, you and your library gain access to the Report Links that
specifically back up this book.
The Publisher will provide access to the Report Links that back up this book and will keep these Report
Links up to date on **www.myreportlinks.com** for five years from the book's first publication date.
We have done our best to make sure all Internet addresses in this book were active and appropriate
when we went to press. However, the author and the Publisher have no control over, and assume
no liability for, the material available on those Internet sites or on other Web sites they may link to.
The usage of the MyReportLinks.com Books Web site is subject to the terms and conditions stated
on the Usage Policy Statement on **www.myreportlinks.com**.
A password may be required to access the Report Links that back up this book. The password is
found on the bottom of page 4 of this book.
Any comments or suggestions can be sent by e-mail to comments@myreportlinks.com or to the
address on the back cover.

Photo Credits: © Corel Corporation, pp. 3, 10; © 1999 PhotoDisc, Inc., pp. 11, 13, 18,
23, 24, 36; Courtesy of America's Story from America's Library/Library of Congress, p. 43;
Courtesy of Famous Texans, p. 15; Courtesy of MyReportLinks.com Books, p. 4; Courtesy
of New Perspectives on the West/PBS, pp. 33, 35, 38; Courtesy of Southwest State Texas
University, p. 16; Courtesy of Texas House of Representatives, p. 25; Courtesy of Texas
Military Forces Museum, p. 41; Courtesy of Texas Parks and Wildlife, p. 20, 29, 31;
Courtesy of the State of Texas, p. 27; Courtesy of The White House, p. 26; Enslow
Publishers, Inc., pp. 1, 17; Library of Congress, p. 3 (Constitution).

Cover Photo: © Corel Corporation.

Cover Description: The Alamo

Tools

Search

Notes

Discuss

▶ MyReportLinks.com Books

Go!

Contents

MyReportLinks.com Books
Great Books, Great Links, Great for Research!

MyReportLinks.com Books present the information you need to learn about your report subject. In addition, they show you where to go on the Internet for more information. The pre-evaluated Report Links that back up this book are kept up to date on **www.myreportlinks.com**. With the purchase of a MyReportLinks.com Books title, you and your library gain access to the Report Links that specifically back up that book. The Report Links save hours of research time and link to dozens—even hundreds—of Web sites, source documents, and photos related to your report topic.

Please see "To Our Readers" on the Copyright page for important information about this book, the MyReportLinks.com Books Web site, and the Report Links that back up this book.

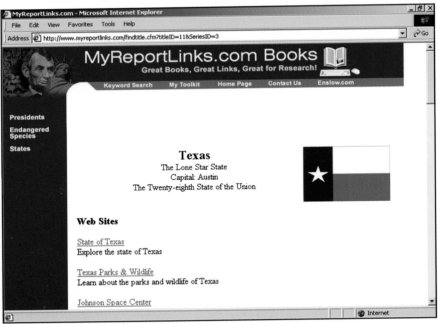

Access:

The Publisher will provide access to the Report Links that back up this book and will try to keep these Report Links up to date on our Web site for five years from the book's first publication date. Please enter **STX2882** if asked for a password.

The Internet sites described below can be accessed at
http://www.myreportlinks.com

▶ **Texas Online**   *EDITOR'S CHOICE
This Web site provides a vast amount of information about Texas.
Links to travel and tourism, recreation, communities, state government,
and much more are included.

Link to this Internet site from http://www.myreportlinks.com

▶ **Texas Parks & Wildlife**   *EDITOR'S CHOICE
At this Web site users can explore parks, historical sites, and wildlife
found in the state of Texas.

Link to this Internet site from http://www.myreportlinks.com

▶ **Johnson Space Center**   *EDITOR'S CHOICE
The Johnson Space Center is located in Houston, Texas. At this Web
site you will learn about shuttle missions, news, facts, and the history
of the Space Center.

Link to this Internet site from http://www.myreportlinks.com

▶ **The Alamo**   *EDITOR'S CHOICE
From the official site for the Alamo, you can learn about the battle and
get information about the building itself.

Link to this Internet site from http://www.myreportlinks.com

▶ **The *Handbook of Texas* Online**   *EDITOR'S CHOICE
The online version of the *New Handbook of Texas* provides a
comprehensive guide to Texas. This virtual encyclopedia contains more
than twenty-three thousand articles about the state's history, geography,
and culture.

Link to this Internet site from http://www.myreportlinks.com

▶ **The Texas Almanac 2004–05**   *EDITOR'S CHOICE
The Texas-Almanac Web site holds information about Texas towns and
cities, culture and arts, environment, history, and other features of Texas.

Link to this Internet site from http://www.myreportlinks.com

Any comments? Contact us: **comments@myreportlinks.com**   5

Report Links

▶ **All About Texas**
This site provides a vast amount of information about Texas. Find out about the Texas Revolution, natural regions in Texas, birds of Texas, and more.

Link to this Internet site from http://www.myreportlinks.com

▶ **Austin City Limits**
At this site you will learn about Austin City Limits, the publicly broad casted television program dedicated to blues, rock, folk, country, and bluegrass music.

Link to this Internet site from http://www.myreportlinks.com

▶ **The Dwight D. Eisenhower Library & Museum**
Find photographs of President Eisenhower, a biography of his life growing up in Texas, information on his military career, and information about the era of his presidency.

Link to this Internet site from http://www.myreportlinks.com

▶ **Famous Texans**
This site holds brief biographies of famous Texans, including Sam Houston, Dan Rather, Roy Orbison, and others

Link to this Internet site from http://www.myreportlinks.com

▶ **Guide to Texas Outside**
This Web site is a guide to the Texas outdoors. Here you will find guides to road trips, hunting and fishing, and sports.

Link to this Internet site from http://www.myreportlinks.com

▶ **LBJ for Kids**
Lyndon Baines Johnson Library and Museum, in Austin, Texas, holds forty-five million pieces of paper donated by LBJ and his family. At this site you can browse through Johnson's papers and learn about the library.

Link to this Internet site from http://www.myreportlinks.com

> The Internet sites described below can be accessed at
> **http://www.myreportlinks.com**

▶**New Perspectives on the West: Texas**
Research the historical importance of some Texas cities, including
San Antonio, Rio Grande, and San Jacinto.

Link to this Internet site from http://www.myreportlinks.com

▶**Office of the Governor: Rick Perry**
Learn about the current Texas governor, and find out information
about the office of the governor and news related to Texas.

Link to this Internet site from http://www.myreportlinks.com

▶**Oveta Culp Hobby**
A native Texan, Oveta Culp Hobby's unprecedented involvement in
government and business made her a pioneer for women in the United
States. Find out about Hobby's life and career.

Link to this Internet site from http://www.myreportlinks.com

▶ **Texas**
America's Story from America's Library, a Library of Congress Web site,
contains an overview of Texas. Learn about the Alamo, Sam Houston,
the Texas Rose, and more.

Link to this Internet site from http://www.myreportlinks.com

▶ **Texas: It's Like a Whole Other Country**
This site provides statistical information about Texas. There are sections
about Texas history, government, parks, libraries, geography, and much more.

Link to this Internet site from http://www.myreportlinks.com

▶ **Texas: It's More Than You Think**
Explore the state of Texas, view images of Texas landscapes, and learn
about Texas culture by navigating through this site.

Link to this Internet site from http://www.myreportlinks.com

Report Links

The Internet sites described below can be accessed at
http://www.myreportlinks.com

▶ **Texas Association of Museums**
This site provides links to many of the museums in Texas.

Link to this Internet site from http://www.myreportlinks.com

▶ **The Texas Constitution**
This online resource includes the entire text of the Texas Constitution.

Link to this Internet site from http://www.myreportlinks.com

▶ **Texas Historical Commission**
The Texas Historical Commission is dedicated to preserving Texas' historic
and prehistoric resources. Become familiar with the commission's projects, as
well as trivia about Texas.

Link to this Internet site from http://www.myreportlinks.com

▶ **Texas Military Forces Museum**
At the Texas Military Forces Museum in Austin, Texas, visitors can learn about
Camp Mabry, the headquarters of the state military forces, the Texas National
Guards, and the history of the Texas military.

Link to this Internet site from http://www.myreportlinks.com

▶ **Texas Ranger Hall of Fame and Museum**
A detailed history of the Texas Rangers law enforcement agency. Browse
through documents, and explore time lines and maps.

Link to this Internet site from http://www.myreportlinks.com

▶ **Texas State Aquarium**
The Texas State Aquarium is dedicated to increasing public understanding
of the Gulf of Mexico. Take a virtual tour of the Gulf and learn about
its inhabitants.

Link to this Internet site from http://www.myreportlinks.com

The Internet sites described below can be accessed at
http://www.myreportlinks.com

▶ **U.S. Census Bureau: Texas QuickFacts**
The official census statistics on the state of Texas can be found at this
Web site. Learn about the population demographics, business and
geography facts, and more.

Link to this Internet site from http://www.myreportlinks.com

▶ **The U.S.-Mexican War: 1846–48**
Experience the Mexican-American War. Learn the history of the war
and about the places where war waged.

Link to this Internet site from http://www.myreportlinks.com

▶ **Welcome to the Texas Governor's Mansion**
At this site you can study the Governor's Mansion in Austin, Texas.
Learn about its history, and find facts and historical information about
the Mansion.

Link to this Internet site from http://www.myreportlinks.com

▶ **The White House**
At the White House Web site for kids, you will find facts about Texas
resident George W. Bush.

Link to this Internet site from http://www.myreportlinks.com

▶ **Wildflower Center**
In 1982, the Wildflower Center was founded by former first lady
Lady Bird Johnson. This Web site lets visitors explore the native
flowers of Texas.

Link to this Internet site from http://www.myreportlinks.com

▶ *World Almanac for Kids Online*
The *World Almanac for Kids Online* Web site provides essential
information about Texas. Here you will learn about the land,
government, education, economy, and the state's history.

Link to this Internet site from http://www.myreportlinks.com

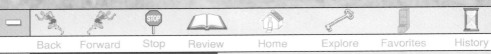
Texas Facts

▶ **Capital**

Austin

▶ **Population**

20,851,820*

▶ **Bird**

Mockingbird

▶ **Fish**

Guadalupe Bass

▶ **Tree**

Pecan

▶ **Flower**

Bluebonnet

▶ **Nickname**

The Lone Star State

Population reflects the 2000 census

▶ **Animal**

Armadillo (small)
Longhorn (large)

▶ **Gemstone**

Blue Topaz

▶ **Insect**

Monarch Butterfly

▶ **Dish**

Chili

▶ **Song**

"Texas, Our Texas"

▶ **Motto**

Friendship

▶ **Flag**

The Lone Star Flag has a blue stripe from top to bottom the width of one third of the flag. In the center of the blue is a white star of five points. The rest of the flag is two equal horizontal stripes of white (above) and red (below).

Origin of the name: Texas, or Tejas (pronounced Te-has), was the Spanish pronunciation of a Caddo people's word meaning "friends" or "allies." Today, Texas citizens are called "Texans." In the early years of settlement and statehood, white settlers were called Texians or Texicans. Hispanic settlers were called Tejanos.[1]

Chapter 1

The State of Texas

Texas is the second largest state in the Union and the largest of the forty-eight continental United States. It has a population of about 21 million, making it the state with the second most people in the United States. Four Texas cities—Austin, Houston, Dallas, and San Antonio—boast over a million people each.[1]

Even though modern transportation has reduced the travel time between various parts of Texas, it is still a big state. The distance from the eastern to the western border in a straight line is over 800 miles.[2] You can drive all day and still be in Texas.

Many Americans think of Texas in terms of cattle drives and oil wells, wide open spaces, Wild West shoot-outs, tough cowboys, and Comanche Indians. Some Texans also still cling to the Wild West image. Rodeos are popular, and barbecue, Tex-Mex, and chicken-fried steak are the favorite foods.

This cowboy statue in ▶ downtown Fort Worth, Texas, is reminiscent of the Wild West.

Many businessmen routinely wear cowboy boots with their suits. Pickup trucks are a favorite means of transportation. Stetson hats, boots, and jeans are popular with men and women throughout the state.

Interesting Places to Visit

Many interesting places in Texas are tied to the state's lively history. The Palo Duro Canyon, southeast of Amarillo, is a miniature Grand Canyon. For 110 miles, steep cliffs drop 800 feet from flat plains to a sheltered valley with a river running through it. In 1874, U.S. Army troops under General Ranald Mackenzie defeated a band of Kiowa Indians on the plains above the canyon. Supposedly, Army troops drove the Kiowa horses over the canyon walls so that the Kiowa could not escape.[3] Later, financier John Adair and legendary rancher Charles Goodnight established the J.A. Ranch in the canyon. Today, the canyon is home to an annual outdoor historical pageant, "Texas," and to some of the state's herds of the well-known longhorn cattle.

In the southwest corner of Texas, on the border with Mexico, Big Bend National Park includes the Chisos Mountains, deep canyons and gorges, the Rio Grande, and a portion of the Chihuahuan Desert. It has been called the "most scenic area of Texas." Big Bend has over a thousand species of plants and a wide variety of animals, reptiles, fish, and birds plus numerous fossil remains.[4]

The Alamo is the site most hallowed by Texans. This former Spanish mission in San Antonio was where, in 1836, for twelve days roughly 189 Texians and Tejanos withstood an assault by thousands of Mexican troops. It was the most famous fight of Texas' war for independence from Mexico. All the defenders were killed. When Sam Houston later led the Texas army to victory in the Battle of

▲ *Large rocket exhibit located just outside the Space Center Houston.*

San Jacinto, one of the battle cries was "Remember the Alamo!" Today, the Daughters of the Republic of Texas operate the mission as a tourist attraction and historic site.

To go from the past to the future, visitors to Texas always want to see Space Center Houston, in Southeast Texas. It offers exhibits, virtual rides, an IMAX theater, and a tram tour that takes guests past rockets and other large outdoor exhibits.

Galveston Island, southeast of Houston, was once the hideout of pirate Jean Laffite. Today it is a tourist attraction on the Gulf of Mexico, with wide beaches, countless seafood restaurants, Victorian homes, and the historic Strand shopping area. Galveston is also home to the University of Texas Medical Branch.

The Metroplex area in North Central Texas is anchored on the east by Dallas and on the west by Fort Worth. The biggest city in between is Arlington, home of

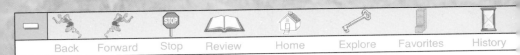

the Texas Rangers baseball team, and the Six Flags Over Texas amusement and water park. Dallas maintains the atmosphere of an eastern, sophisticated city and is home to the famous Dallas Cowboys football team. Fort Worth clings to its Old West history and proudly calls itself Cowtown. Visitors can go back in time by strolling through the Stockyards National Historic District. The city also boasts one of the finest complexes of small museums in the country.

Politics

Texas breeds politicians. One of the most famous was Sam Houston. After the Battle of San Jacinto, Houston was twice president of the Republic of Texas and later a U.S. senator and governor of the state. President Dwight D. Eisenhower was born in Texas, although he did not live there much. President Lyndon B. Johnson used his Texas drawl and Texas ways effectively as president. And President George W. Bush, though born in Maine, grew up in Midland, Texas.

Famous Texans

Three Texas men set the tone for much of Texas literature between World War II and the 1960s. They were folklorist J. Frank Dobie, historian Walter Prescott Webb, and naturalist Roy Bedichek. They wrote about a land of cattle, boots, and strong, fearless men. In the 1970s, author Larry McMurtry called for the state to turn from rural literature to one based in cities, reflecting the state's culture at that time. But he later wrote the best-selling *Lonesome Dove*, a trail-drive and cowboy novel. Today, Elmer Kelton is one of the best-known novelists who writes of both the old and new West. Sportswriter Dan Jenkins is another Texan who has written frequently about his home state.

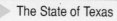

Alvin Ailey - Microsoft Internet Explorer   _ □ ×

e Edit View Favorites Tools Help

dress 🗎 http://www.famoustexans.com/dobie.htm   ⟳ Go Links »

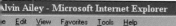

J. Frank Dobie

J. Frank Dobie, (1888-1964) folklorist, was born on a ranch in Live Oak County, Texas, on September 26, 1888, the eldest of six ldren of Richard J. and Ella (Byler) Dobie. His ranching heritage became an early uence on his character and personality. His fundamentalist father read the Bible to ank and the other five children, and his mother read them "Ivanhoe" and introduced m to "The Scottish Chiefs", "Pilgrim's Progress", and "Swiss Family Robinson". He the ranch when he was sixteen and moved to Alice, where he lived with his ndparents and finished high school. In 1906 he enrolled in Southwestern University Georgetown, where he met Bertha McKee, whom he married in 1916, and ofessor Albert Shipp Pegues, his English teacher, who introduced him to English etry, particularly the Romantics, and encouraged him as a writer. Dobie's education a teacher and writer continued after graduation in 1910. He worked two summers a reporter, first for the "San Antonio Express" and then the "Galveston Tribune". He got his first teaching job 1910 in Alpine, where he was also the principal, play director, and editor of the school paper. He returned to orgetown in 1911 and taught in the Southwestern University preparatory school until 1913, when he went to lumbia to work on his master's degree. With his new M.A. he joined the University of Texas faculty in 1914. this time he also joined the Texas Folklore Society. Dobie left the university in 1917 and served for two years he field artillery in World War I. His outfit was sent overseas right at the war's end, and he returned to be scharged in 1919. In 1919 he published his first articles. He resigned his position at the university in 1920 to anage his uncle Jim Dobie's ranch. During this year on the Rancho de Los Olmos with the vaqueros and the ck and the land that had been part of his formation, Dobie discovered his calling - to transmute all the nness of this life and land and culture into literature. The Texas Folklore Society was the main avenue for his w mission, and the University of Texas library with all its Texas resources was his vehicle.

one   🌐 Internet

▲ *J. Frank Dobie became famous for his writings on the culture of Texas and the Southwest. He retold stories about cowboys, longhorn cattle, and other people and animals of the range country.*

Texas today has Tejano writers of note in Rolando Hinojosa, Sandra Cisneros, and Dagoberto Gilb. Henry Cisneros was the first Hispanic-American mayor of a major city—San Antonio—and later became secretary of the U.S. Department of Housing and Urban Development.

Texas women have accomplished much. Adina DeZavala is credited with saving the Alamo from destruction. She was the daughter of a former Mexican official who sided with Texas when it fought for independence. In 1908, DeZavala barricaded herself in the Alamo, drawing national attention to the need to stop it from being torn down.

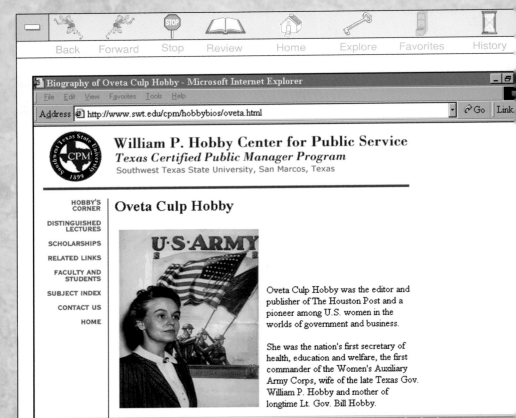

Biography of Oveta Culp Hobby - Microsoft Internet Explorer

File Edit View Favorites Tools Help

Address http://www.swt.edu/cpm/hobbybios/oveta.html   Go Link

William P. Hobby Center for Public Service
Texas Certified Public Manager Program
Southwest Texas State University, San Marcos, Texas

HOBBY'S CORNER
DISTINGUISHED LECTURES
SCHOLARSHIPS
RELATED LINKS
FACULTY AND STUDENTS
SUBJECT INDEX
CONTACT US
HOME

Oveta Culp Hobby

Oveta Culp Hobby was the editor and publisher of The Houston Post and a pioneer among U.S. women in the worlds of government and business.

She was the nation's first secretary of health, education and welfare, the first commander of the Women's Auxiliary Army Corps, wife of the late Texas Gov. William P. Hobby and mother of longtime Lt. Gov. Bill Hobby.

Internet

▲ Oveta Culp Hobby pioneered for women's rights in the fields of government and business.

German-born sculptress Elisabet Ney created the statues of Sam Houston and Stephen F. Austin that grace the state's capitol building. Oveta Culp Hobby was owner and publisher of the *Houston Post*. During World War II, she was in charge of the Women's Army Corps (WAC). Later, President Eisenhower appointed her to lead the Department of Health, Education and Welfare. Barbara Jordan was the first African-American woman admitted to the Texas bar. She later served in both the Texas and the federal legislatures in the 1960s and 1970s. Texas was also the birthplace of Babe Didrikson Zaharias, perhaps the greatest woman athlete of the 1900s.

Chapter 2 ▶

Land and Climate

Texas falls easily into four natural regions. In the southwest corner, the mountains and canyons of Big Bend mark the *Trans-Pecos*. The high plains take in the Panhandle and a swatch of land stretching south, ending in the Edwards Plateau, where plains have eroded into Texas' famous Hill Country. Within the high plains, the Cap Rock

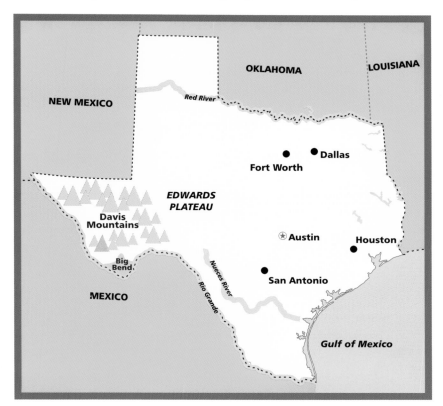

▲ A map of Texas.

▲ *Situated on the Mexican border, Big Bend National Park is a place where countries and cultures meet. With its diverse environment of desert, mountains, and canyons, it is an ideal travel destination.*

Escarpment divides the southern high plains from the staked plains of the Panhandle, or the *Llano Estacado*, as the Spanish called the area. Many think the name comes from the layered look of the Cap Rock, but some historians suggest that Francisco Coronado's expedition may have staked their route across the sea of grass so that they could find their way back.[1]

Rolling plains cover the north central part of the state. Near Dallas is the area once known as the *Grand Prairie* (there is still a town by that name). The eastern and western Cross Timbers consist of two narrow strips of oak and other hardwood trees, separated sometimes by as much as a hundred miles by the Grand Prairie.[2] Finally, the *Coastal Plains* run the length of East Texas and are significantly more lush and green than the high plains.

In West Texas, where winds come from the desert areas of northern Mexico, average rainfall is less than eight inches per year. This part of Texas created the generally accepted picture of the state as a land of bare, brown earth.[3]

In lush and green East Texas, rainfall can be over fifty-five inches a year. Here the winds sweep up and over the waters of the Gulf of Mexico, bringing heavy moisture with them.[4] The Big Thicket in Southeast Texas is an area with heavy growth of trees and underbrush. There is a large population of deer, bobcats, coyotes, and birds. Today the Big Thicket is much smaller than it once was because the logging industry has harvested trees and made the size of the preserve smaller. To the north, the Piney Woods, a belt of pine and hardwood trees, is the source of most commercial lumber in Texas.

▶ Weather

The highest temperature ever recorded in Texas is 120°F in Seymour (North Central Texas) in 1936 and in Monahans (Southwest Texas) in 1994. The lowest recorded temperature is −23°F at Tulia (near the Panhandle) in 1899 and at Seminole in 1933.[5]

Parts of Texas can suffer unbearably hot summers, like that of 1980 when the temperature in North Central Texas topped 100°F for forty-two days in a row.[6] Winters are also fierce. Devastating "northers" blow through the Panhandle into Central Texas, dropping the temperature thirty degrees within minutes.

▶ Natural Disasters

Several major hurricanes have hit areas near the Gulf Coast. The Galveston storm of 1900 killed over six thousand people. It is still the worst natural disaster ever to

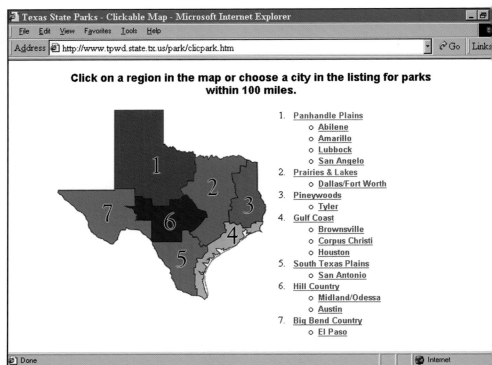

Click on a region in the map or choose a city in the listing for parks within 100 miles.

1. Panhandle Plains
   o Abilene
   o Amarillo
   o Lubbock
   o San Angelo
2. Prairies & Lakes
   o Dallas/Fort Worth
3. Pineywoods
   o Tyler
4. Gulf Coast
   o Brownsville
   o Corpus Christi
   o Houston
5. South Texas Plains
   o San Antonio
6. Hill Country
   o Midland/Odessa
   o Austin
7. Big Bend Country
   o El Paso

▲ This interactive map shows the many different travel regions Texas has to offer.

have hit the United States. Hurricanes bring heavy rains and destructive winds as far north as the Metroplex. The Valley—the land near the Rio Grande border with Texas—is generally milder. Because of its long growing season, the Valley is known for grapefruit and other fruit crops.

Texas is at the southwest end of the Tornado Belt. Most tornadoes occur in April, May, and June. Sometimes more than one hundred tornadoes touchdown in a year. In the Central Texas town of Jarrell, a storm killed twenty-seven people, shattered houses, and pulled asphalt off roads in May 1997.[7]

Economy

The Texas economy set new records in the late 1990s. Most Texans had a higher average standard of living than most other United States residents. Employment and new construction were at all-time highs. The cost of living rose less than in previous years, annual personal income grew, and mortgage rates dropped. If Texas were still an independent nation, it would be the eleventh largest economy in the world.[1]

The rest of the United States—and the world—has long thought of Texas as a rich land.[2] Not all Texans are rich. Throughout the state's history, many Texans have been quite poor.[3]

▶ Tough Times

When Texas was a Mexican province, residents were dependent on the Mexican government for their services and supplies. Most Texans were poor farmers. In the mid-nineteenth century, slave-owning planters established large plantations in East Texas. They raised cotton for export to Europe. They made their money in foreign countries, and they spent it there. They did not spend it in Texas, so there was no real economy in the state. Cotton remained the main cash crop through the Civil War era (1861–65). The plantation owners lost the basis of their flourishing economy when they could no longer own and use slaves.

Farming

Small farmers moved to the west, but the Texas landscape is not kind to small farmers. Because the land is dry and does not grow crops easily, it is difficult to make much money unless one owns large portions of land.

The cattle industry in Texas developed after the Civil War. Cattle had been in Texas since the days of the Spanish conquistadors, but until the 1860s there was little market for them. Illinois merchant Joseph G. McCoy worked out a plan whereby a railroad was extended west to Abilene, Kansas. Soon other "railhead" towns developed. The towns had corrals, tanks, loading chutes, and everything needed to ship cattle. Texas ranchers drove cattle, all longhorns, north to these new markets. Some ranchers got their cattle free by rounding up strays that had lived in the chaparral and mesquite thickets of South Texas for generations. A longhorn might cost three or four dollars in Texas. The same animal brought ten times that much when driven north to be shipped east by rail. Trail drives gave rise to a colorful national figure—the cowboy. The trail-drive era came to an end because farmers settled the open land, barbed wire fenced it off, and northerners developed a taste for cattle less chewy than the longhorn. Other problems included overstocking, owners not attending to their herds, and severe winters.

The Oil Industry

In the early twentieth century, oil became the driving force of the Texas economy. The first important oil well gushed in at Spindletop in Southeast Texas in 1901. By the 1920s, vast oil fields were discovered in the Permian Basin of West Texas. Ranchers who were rich in land suddenly also became rich in cash when oil was found on their land.

▲ *An oil pump in Texas.*

Then fields were found in West and North Central Texas. In 1930, an independent oil explorer (called a wildcatter) named Columbus M. "Dad" Joiner brought in a drill he had named Daisy Bradford No. 3 well near Kilgore. This opened the large East Texas fields.

Until World War II, the Texas economy was based on products the land produced—cotton, cattle, oil, pecans, and timber. Most Texans still lived on farms and ranches. After World War II, many Texans moved to the cities. Family farms were abandoned because people could not make a living on them.

In the 1970s, the Texas economy flourished because of a demand for petroleum. Many Texans made fortunes in oil. Real estate boomed. Then in the mid-1980s, the oil-based economy of the state bottomed out due to over-production, dropping prices, and the import of oil from foreign countries. Texas had drilled its oil at a fast pace, without conserving for the future. In addition, the oil

industry had significantly polluted the environment.[4]
Many fortunes were lost. Office buildings stood empty,
and oil-drilling rigs were silent. Today, there is renewed
interest in drilling for Texas oil.

High-tech industries have moved into the state,
principally in the Austin area, and one fourth of all Texans
working in manufacturing are employed by high-tech
(computer) industries. Agriculture has suffered because of
a long drought, but housing construction, transportation,
and communication industries are growing, as are finan-
cial institutions and the insurance and real estate businesses.
The Dallas/Fort Worth Metroplex, Austin, and the
Houston area successfully compete for large national
companies, such as Burlington Northern, Dell Computers,
Motorola, etc. But Texas still produces oil and coal
products, food products, and transportation equipment.
Its principal farm crops are cattle, cotton, dairy products,
and nursery or greenhouse plants.

▲ Houston is undergoing rapid development in the areas of finance
and real estate.

Government

The capital of Texas is Austin. Texas state government, like the federal government, is divided into executive, legislative, and judicial branches. The governor serves a four-year term. The office of governor does not have as much power as in some other states.[1] The legislative veto is the governor's strongest political tool. Unofficially the governor influences government at all levels and is always a strong

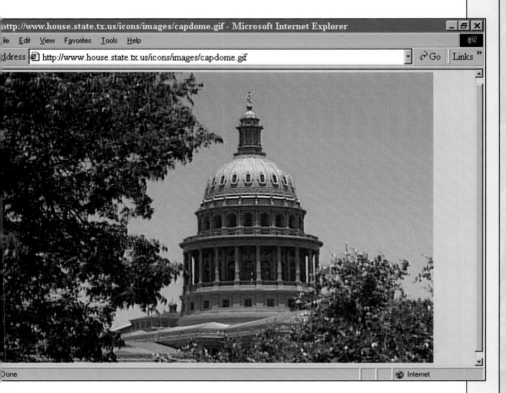

The Texas Capitol building is located in Austin.

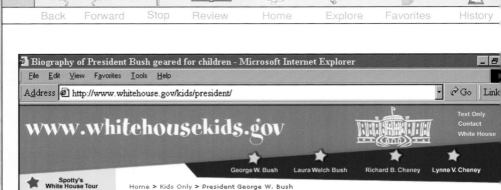

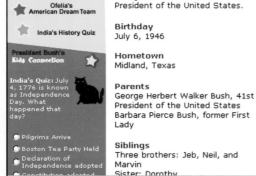

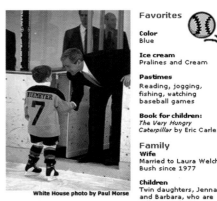

▲ *President George W. Bush greets a young hockey player.*

leader of his or her political party. The governor appoints the secretary of state. The governor also appoints one of the most powerful persons in the state, the secretary of the Railroad Commission. That body controls oil and natural gas production. Elected officials, all with a term of four years, include the lieutenant governor, attorney general, comptroller of public accounts, commissioner of the general land office, and commissioner of agriculture.[2]

▶ Texas Legislature

There are 181 members of the Texas legislature, thirty-one in the senate and one hundred fifty in the House of Representatives. The legislature opens its session on the second Tuesday of January in odd-numbered years and continues until May. The governor may call special sessions.

Texas is governed by a constitution adopted in 1876. Over four hundred amendments have been attached to this constitution to make it more appropriate for an urban, modern state. In the 1970s, some legislators called for constitutional revisions that would have given the governor more power, called for annual sessions of the legislature, reorganized the judiciary system (judges are now elected), and reformed county government. Voters rejected the revisions.[3] Today, the constitution is over six times the length of the U.S. Constitution.[4]

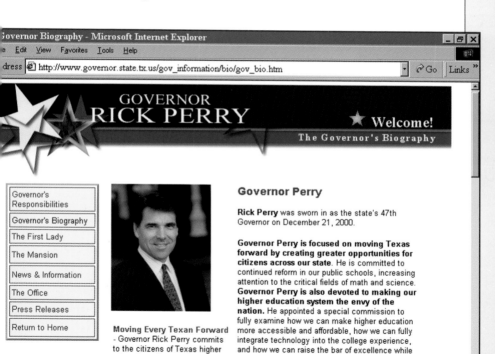

Governor Biography - Microsoft Internet Explorer

File Edit View Favorites Tools Help

Address http://www.governor.state.tx.us/gov_information/bio/gov_bio.htm   Go   Links

GOVERNOR
RICK PERRY   ★ Welcome!
                    The Governor's Biography

- Governor's Responsibilities
- Governor's Biography
- The First Lady
- The Mansion
- News & Information
- The Office
- Press Releases
- Return to Home

Moving Every Texan Forward - Governor Rick Perry commits to the citizens of Texas higher education reform and expanded opportunities to succeed.

Governor Perry

Rick Perry was sworn in as the state's 47th Governor on December 21, 2000.

Governor Perry is focused on moving Texas forward by creating greater opportunities for citizens across our state. He is committed to continued reform in our public schools, increasing attention to the critical fields of math and science. **Governor Perry is also devoted to making our higher education system the envy of the nation.** He appointed a special commission to fully examine how we can make higher education more accessible and affordable, how we can fully integrate technology into the college experience, and how we can raise the bar of excellence while meeting the evolving workforce needs of our state.

▲ Rick Perry became governor of Texas after the former governor, George W. Bush, was elected president of the United States.

Shifts in Politics

The political landscape of Texas saw many changes in the last decades of the twentieth century. By the 1980s, women and minorities—African Americans, Hispanic Americans, and Asian Americans—had a strong presence in the legislature. By 1998, these minorities constituted 45 percent of the state's voting population.[5] Also by the late 1990s, the Republican Party held control in this traditionally Democratic state. The Republicans were helped to power by the Sharpstown scandal of the mid-1980s. Prominent Democratic office holders were convicted of promoting legislation by which they gained illegal stock profits. In addition, political power in Texas shifted from the urban areas, which are usually Democratic, to the Republican suburbs. In 1998, George W. Bush was reelected governor by a landslide. He carried with him Republican candidates for most major offices, including legislators and judges. Bush's move to the presidency of the United States may affect the Texas Republican Party. Rick Perry, the first Republican lieutenant governor in Texas in over a hundred years, succeeded Bush.

History

The Spanish were the first Europeans to explore Texas. They came to a land occupied by American Indians—the warlike Karankawa, the peaceful Caddo, as well as Apache, the Comanche and Kiowa, the Tonkawa, the Jumano, and other smaller tribes.

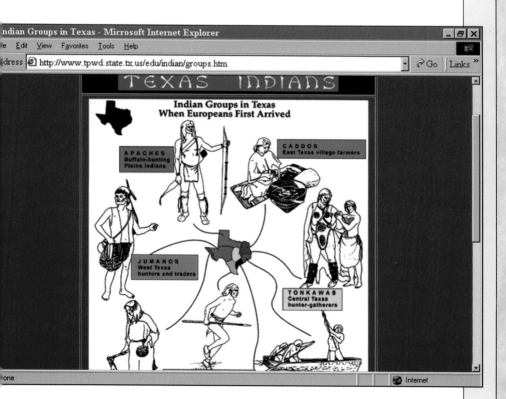

▲ When the first Spaniards arrived in Texas, many different American Indian tribes were already living there. Some of these included the Apache, Jumano, Tonkawa, and Coahuiltecan.

▶ Newcomers

Spanish explorer Alvar Núñez Cabeza de Vaca and his men were shipwrecked on the Texas Gulf Coast in 1528. Cabeza de Vaca spent six years in Texas and was the first European to cross the land. Sometimes he wandered on foot and was lost. Sometimes the Karankawa Indians held him prisoner.

Conquistador (Spanish for conqueror) Francisco Vásquez de Coronado was the next important Spaniard in Texas, arriving with an expedition force in 1540. He searched for the Seven Cities of Cibola thought to exist in what is now the American Southwest. He was looking for gold, but he found only pueblos. The American Indians were at first friendly but soon learned to distrust Coronado. Eventually he killed many of the natives.

The friars (Catholic missionaries) followed in the late 1700s and established missions. The Spanish were determined to conquer the land and convert the native population to Christianity. The oldest surviving settlement in Texas is the Franciscan mission at Ysleta on the Rio Grande near present-day El Paso. The Spanish also established military garrisons, or *presidios*, such as LaBahia, near present-day Goliad, to support the missions. In 1718, they established Mission San Antonio de Valero on the San Antonio River. The nearby presidio was San Antonio de Bexar. By 1800, the three largest population centers in Texas were Bexar (now San Antonio), LaBahia, and Nacogdoches in East Texas.[1]

▶ "The Mother of Texas"

By 1800, farmers, shopkeepers, and tradesmen from the United States had drifted in. So did land-seeking adventurers, often called filibusters. Philip Nolan, a horse trader, built a

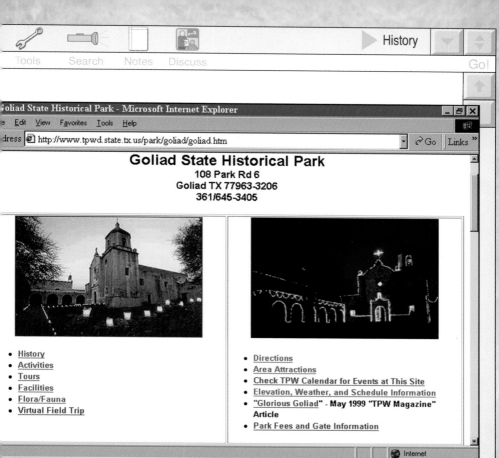

Goliad State Historical Park
108 Park Rd 6
Goliad TX 77963-3206
361/645-3405

- History
- Activities
- Tours
- Facilities
- Flora/Fauna
- Virtual Field Trip

- Directions
- Area Attractions
- Check TPW Calendar for Events at This Site
- Elevation, Weather, and Schedule Information
- "Glorious Goliad" - May 1999 "TPW Magazine" Article
- Park Fees and Gate Information

▲ *Due to its strategic position, Goliad played a major role in the Texas Revolution. Located on the San Antonio River, the Goliad State Historical Park features a replica of Mission Nuestra Senora del Espiritu Santo de Zuniga.*

fort in Central Texas. Suspecting he wanted to steal land and power, the Spanish attacked the fort and killed him.[2] James Long was a merchant and doctor who organized a group to fight for Texas' freedom. In 1820, he left his wife behind at Point Bolivar on the Gulf Coast when he tried to seize the mission at LaBahia. A Spanish force captured him and sent him to Mexico, where he was killed by a guard. Jane Long is often mistakenly thought to have given birth to the first white child born in Texas in 1821. She is therefore called the "Mother of Texas."[3]

▶ "The Father of Texas"

Since about 1800, Spain had offered land grants to Americans settling in Texas, on the condition that the new-comers swear allegiance to Spain and convert to the Catholic faith. The immigrants were sponsored by *empresarios*. These colonizers could buy Texas land at bargain prices—12.5 cents an acre.[4] The most famous empresario was Moses Austin, who came from Missouri in 1820. After he died, his son Stephen took over the land grant. Stephen F. Austin is called the "Father of Texas" because of his work encouraging Anglo-American settlement and independence from Mexico.[5]

▶ The Texas Revolution

Texas was part of the Mexican province of *Coahuila y Texas*. The government of Mexico had total power over the settlers and exercised it suddenly and without notice. There was no trial by jury, bail, freedom of speech, or free-dom to petition. Settlers clashed with the government over title to their land, tariffs and customs, and immigration.

The Texas Revolution began with isolated incidents. In 1825, U.S. President John Quincy Adams appointed Joel Poinsett minister to Mexico. Adams authorized him to offer Mexico one million dollars for Texas. Mexico had always been afraid the United States wanted Texas. The government refused the offer. In 1826, an empresario named Haden Edwards caused Mexico so much trouble that his land grant was taken away. Edwards then declared his grant in East Texas the free state of Fredonia. Mexico sent armed forces to put down the rebellion, but Edwards had already fled.[6]

When Mexico proclaimed an end to slavery and tried to relocate convicts to Texas, the spirit of rebellion spread

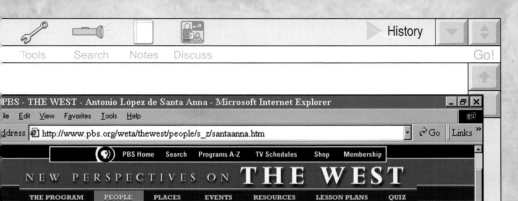

PBS - THE WEST - Antonio López de Santa Anna - Microsoft Internet Explorer

File Edit View Favorites Tools Help

Address http://www.pbs.org/weta/thewest/people/s_z/santaanna.htm   Go   Links »

PBS Home   Search   Programs A-Z   TV Schedules   Shop   Membership

NEW PERSPECTIVES ON THE WEST

THE PROGRAM   PEOPLE   PLACES   EVENTS   RESOURCES   LESSON PLANS   QUIZ

PEOPLE

-C

-H

-R

-Z

Sacagawea
Santa Anna, Antonio López de
Seguín, Juan
Serra, Father Junípero
Sheridan, Philip
Sherman, William
Tecumseh
Singleton, Benjamin "Pap"
Sitting Bull
Smith, Joseph
Stanford, Leland
Strauss, Levi
Sutter, John

Antonio López de Santa Anna

(1794-1876)

The dominant figure in Mexican politics for much of the 19th century, Antonio López de Santa Anna left a legacy of disappointment and disaster by consistently placing his own self-interest above his duty to the nation.

Born in the state of Vera Cruz in 1794, Santa Anna embarked on his long career in the army at age 16 as a cadet. He fought for a time for the Spanish against Mexican independence, but along with many other army officers switched sides in 1821 to help install Augustin de Iturbide as head of state of an independent Mexico.

Mexico was a highly fractured and chaotic nation for much of its first century of independence, in no small part due to the machinations of men such as Santa Anna. In 1828 he used his military influence to lift the losing candidate into the presidency, being rewarded in turn with appointment as the highest-ranking general in the land. His reputation and influence were further strengthened by his critical role in defeating an 1829 Spanish effort to reconquer their former colony.

Internet

▲ Antonio López de Santa Anna was a very powerful military leader who sought public recognition and acclaim more than money. His appreciation for Mexico led him to defend his country during the Mexican War.

throughout the settlements. Stephen F. Austin took a petition to Mexico City. The document presented the settlers' requests for separation from Coahuila, and other matters. Austin met successfully with Mexican President Antonio López de Santa Anna and was headed back to Texas. He was then arrested, returned to Mexico City, and imprisoned. He was released on Christmas Day, 1834.

▶ "Napoleon of the West"

William Barret Travis led a small group of Texians to capture a seacoast fort at Anahuac. Travis initially took

Mexican soldiers prisoner, then released them to return to Mexico. But General Martin Perfecto de Cos, military commander of northern Mexico, demanded the surrender of Travis and his "outlaws." Cos and his troops occupied San Antonio. An informal Texian army began to assemble to defy the Mexicans. The Texians defeated Cos's troops in battles at Gonzales and at Bexar. Cos and his troops left Texas with the promise never to return. Santa Anna, often called the "Napoleon of the West," was angry at the Texian defiance. He sent an army of fifteen hundred soldiers under General Jose Urrea to capture Goliad. The president himself led a troop of six thousand to eliminate the Americans in Texas.

The Alamo

General Sam Houston, in charge of the Texian army, had sent James Bowie to San Antonio de Bexar to hold the city against the Mexicans. Travis and an army of hunter-trappers, not professional soldiers, joined Bowie. Bowie estimated they needed a thousand men to defend the Alamo, the former mission in which they established their headquarters. Houston expected Bowie to abandon the mission, but he did not. Travis wrote "To The People of Texas and All Americans in the World" asking for more men. Travis vowed his men would fight until death. Davy Crockett of Tennessee, a dozen Tennessee sharpshooters, and thirty-five men from Gonzales, Texas, slipped through the lines to the Alamo. The Texians held the Mexicans off for thirteen days but were finally killed and their bodies burned in a large fire. Tradition says 189 men died defending the Alamo. Some historians today think the number is closer to 250.

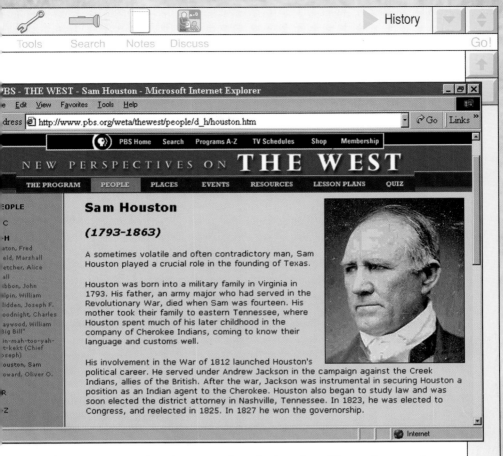

PBS - THE WEST - Sam Houston - Microsoft Internet Explorer

File Edit View Favorites Tools Help

Address http://www.pbs.org/weta/thewest/people/d_h/houston.htm   Go   Links

PBS Home   Search   Programs A-Z   TV Schedules   Shop   Membership

NEW PERSPECTIVES ON THE WEST

THE PROGRAM   PEOPLE   PLACES   EVENTS   RESOURCES   LESSON PLANS   QUIZ

Sam Houston

(1793-1863)

A sometimes volatile and often contradictory man, Sam Houston played a crucial role in the founding of Texas.

Houston was born into a military family in Virginia in 1793. His father, an army major who had served in the Revolutionary War, died when Sam was fourteen. His mother took their family to eastern Tennessee, where Houston spent much of his later childhood in the company of Cherokee Indians, coming to know their language and customs well.

His involvement in the War of 1812 launched Houston's political career. He served under Andrew Jackson in the campaign against the Creek Indians, allies of the British. After the war, Jackson was instrumental in securing Houston a position as an Indian agent to the Cherokee. Houston also began to study law and was soon elected the district attorney in Nashville, Tennessee. In 1823, he was elected to Congress, and reelected in 1825. In 1827 he won the governorship.

Sam Houston played a major role in the founding of Texas. As general of the Texian army, he fought and defeated Santa Anna's troops.

Houston gathered an army in Gonzales. He expected General James Fannin's force to join him with almost five hundred men. But Urrea met Fannin at Goliad, and the much larger Mexican army defeated Fannin's men. Fannin surrendered his troops on the condition that his men would be treated honorably. Instead, 342 men were executed. Twenty-eight escaped.

While the Alamo was under attack, a delegation of fifty-seven Texians met at Washington-on-the-Brazos on March 2, 1836. They declared independence from Mexico and drafted a constitution. Today Texans observe the anniversary, March 2, as Texas Independence Day. After

the fall of the Alamo and the massacre at Goliad, Houston was criticized for marching east instead of standing to fight. Houston retreated because he knew his rag-tag army was not ready to face the overwhelming numbers of the Mexican army. Frightened civilians along his path fled their homes. They took with them whatever they could carry. It was spring, roads were muddy, and rivers were flooding. This miserable civilian flight became known as the Runaway Scrape.

▶ Texas Achieves Independence

Houston's troops turned and fought the Mexican army under Santa Anna at San Jacinto (near present-day Houston) on April 21. The Texians attacked at 3:30 P.M. The Mexicans were resting in preparation for the battle they expected the

▲ *The Alamo was established in 1718 as the first Spanish mission to Christianize and educate native peoples. Once its mission role was completed, the old buildings were abandoned and the site became known as the "cradle of Texas liberty" during the revolution.*

next morning. In the eighteen-minute battle, Houston lost nine men. Santa Anna lost 630 men; 208 Mexican soldiers were wounded and 730 captured. Santa Anna, disguised as a peasant, was captured the next day. Houston resisted his men's request to execute Santa Anna. He sent Santa Anna to Washington, D.C. There, Andrew Jackson exiled him to Cuba. On May 14, Santa Anna signed the Treaty of Velasco, which led to Texas' independence.[7] Eventually, Santa Anna was allowed to return to his homeland.

Spanish/Mexican authority over Texas ended on that battlefield, but the influence lingers in food, architectural features, sports (rodeo), and religion. Every major river in Texas bears a Spanish name, which the exception of the Red River on the northern border of the state.[8]

In 1835, "The Consultation," then the official government of Texas, created the Texas Rangers to protect the Texas frontier against American Indian raids. The Rangers became a division of the Texas State Department of Public Safety in 1935.

▶ A New Republic

General elections were held in September 1836. In 1837, the Republic of Texas capital was established at the city of Houston. Sam Houston was president. The new government had no money, an undisciplined army, problems with Mexico, and troubles with American Indians on its frontiers. President Houston thought statehood would help them deal with these problems. The U.S. government would not grant statehood because Texas would enter the Union as a slave state. That would give slave states power in the federal legislature at a time when the country was bitterly divided over slavery. The United States also did

not want to deal with Texas' continuing border troubles with Mexico.

According to the constitution, Houston could not succeed himself as president. The second president, Mirabeau B. Lamar, showed no interest in statehood. He moved the capital from Houston to Austin. To give the government money, Lamar printed paper dollars, called redbacks, that drove the republic $5 million into debt.[9]

When Lamar's term expired, Houston was reelected in 1841. The U.S. government was by then interested in annexing Texas as a state. Anson L. Jones, fourth president of Texas, brought Texas into the United States. During his

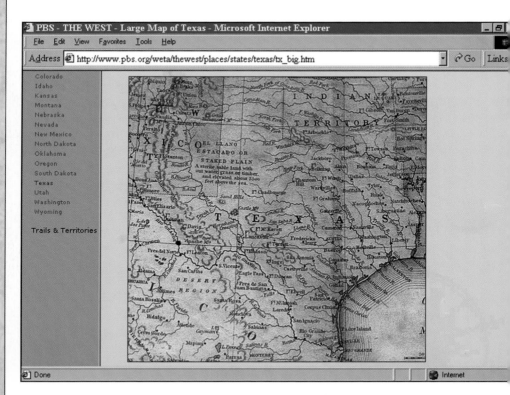

▲ This map shows the often disputed border between Texas and Mexico.

administration, Texas legislators voted to reject proposals from Mexico that Texas remain independent and accept a United States offer. Texas formally became a state on December 29, 1845.[10] Sam Houston and Thomas J. Rusk were elected as the first U.S. senators from Texas.

Texas now had U.S. support in its ongoing border troubles with Mexico. In 1846, Congress declared war on Mexico over border issues. Texas' boundaries were finally settled by the Compromise of 1850.

The Civil War

When the Civil War began, the Texas legislature and voters in East Texas were in favor of joining the Confederate States of America. Sam Houston held out against seceding from the Union. He had the support of settlers in western and central Texas. As governor of Texas, he was asked to swear an oath of allegiance to the Confederacy. He refused and was removed from office. Most Texas men between the ages of sixteen and sixty left home to fight.[11]

Galveston was blockaded, which caused great economic hardship because shipments of necessary goods could not arrive. During the 1863 Battle of Sabine Pass on the Gulf Coast, forty-two men with six cannons turned back a Union invasion fleet of twenty ships and three gunboats.[12] But no major battles of the Civil War were fought on Texas soil. Yet the last battle was. Just over a month after the Confederacy had surrendered, Union and Confederate forces clashed at the Battle of Palmito Ranch. The Confederacy won a decisive victory in what was a meaningless battle.

Still, there was unrest in Texas. Southerners who had not gone to war were on the alert to find those still loyal to the Union. In the most famous case, forty men were

hung at Gainesville, in North Central Texas, for loyalty to the Union. The state had even more trouble with the Comanche and Kiowa tribes. The tribes began to raid small communities because they knew the men of fighting age were away at war.

Reconstruction

Like most other southern states, Texas lost control of its government during Reconstruction, the period after the defeat of the Confederacy. General lawlessness in Texas included American Indian attacks, outlaws who roamed the state freely, and vigilante attacks against Union loyalists and African Americans. In 1867, Congress passed the strict Military Reconstruction Act and placed Texas under the control of General Phil Sheridan.[13] Government officials were appointed by the federal government, and the state constitution was nullified. Texas did not really take over its own government again until 1874.[14]

The Oil Boom

In North Texas, farmers fought drought, grasshoppers, prairie fires, and blizzards. Their main crop was cotton, while ranchers kept huge herds of beef cattle. In East Texas, fortunes were made in lumber.

The economic face of Texas changed with the discovery of oil. By 1900, oil was needed to fuel engines, light lanterns, and lubricate machinery. The oil boom lasted through the 1920s. Boomtowns sprang up on the oil fields. The Panhandle town of Borger, for instance, attracted forty-five thousand people in eight months. People lived in tents, shacks, trailers, and autos with unpaved streets, unclean water, and other hardships. There was no law and order. Thievery and murder were common. Yet by 1928, Texas led the nation in oil production.[15]

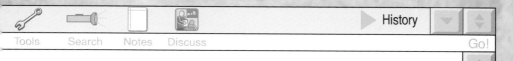

World War I

When the United States entered World War I in 1917, Texans enthusiastically supported the federal government. Large numbers of soldiers trained in the state, particularly pilots in the new field of aviation. Almost two hundred thousand Texans served in the armed forces. The war era was also a time of women's suffrage and prohibition. Racial discrimination was widespread. Governor James "Farmer" Ferguson ran on a 1914 ticket that claimed to ignore the conflict over prohibition (making alcoholic beverages illegal). He was opposed to racial discrimination, but in his second term he was impeached for misuse

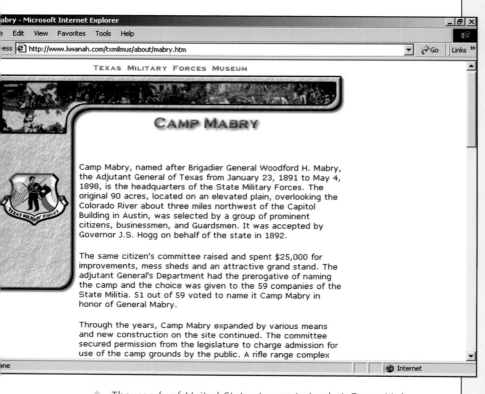

Thousands of United States troops trained at Camp Mabry before leaving to fight in World War I.

of funds, including accepting money from breweries. In 1925, his wife, Miriam "Ma" Ferguson, became the first woman ever elected governor of a state. "Farmer" Ferguson is generally considered to have run the state during his wife's tenure in office.

The Great Depression and the Dust Bowl

The Depression in Texas was made worse by the Dust Bowl, a phenomenon caused by bad farming practices that also affected Oklahoma, Colorado, Kansas, and New Mexico. Drought, overgrazing, grasshoppers, and plowing natural grasses had made the earth dry and loose. When the wind blew—as it did constantly—it caused dust storms so severe that people could not see their hands in front of their faces. Because of the Dust Bowl, more people left the failing family farms to settle in cities.

World War II

During World War II, the state was home to 15 army training bases, and over 40 air bases. One such base was Randolph Field, where every pilot went for basic training. This time it also housed several large prisoner-of-war camps, holding soldiers from Germany and Italy, as well as displaced Japanese-American citizens. Dallas, Fort Worth, San Antonio, and Houston grew because of war-related industries. Houston developed as one of the major petrochemical (oil-related industries) centers in the nation.

Desegregation

Following the war, the state legislature tried to improve education, the prison system, and mental hospitals. In the 1950s, desegregation of schools caused major conflict. In 1956, the Texas Rangers were sent to restore order in

Mansfield, a small community southwest of Fort Worth. No African-American students registered that day.[16] Eventually, however, schools were integrated by court order in the 1960s and 1970s. In that same period, integration came to most public facilities, from golf courses to lunch counters.

▶ Famous Crimes of the Twentieth Century

In the 1960s, Texas saw two crimes that horrified the nation. In 1963, President John F. Kennedy was assassinated as he rode in an open car in a welcoming parade in Dallas. The lone gunman was Lee Harvey Oswald. His motives are still unclear.

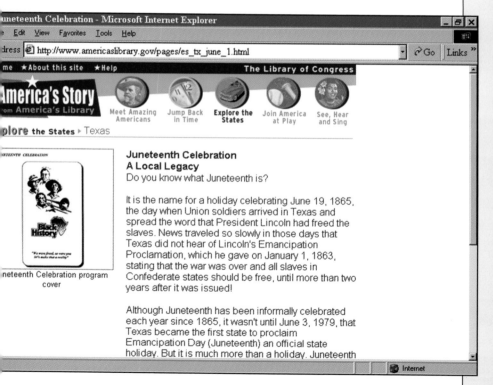

▲ In 1979, Texas became the first state to declare Juneteenth Day, or Emancipation Day, an official state holiday.

In August 1966, University of Texas student Charles Whitman went to the top of the library tower in Austin carrying six guns and ammunition. Once a Marine sharpshooter, Whitman killed seventeen and wounded thirty before a policeman killed him.[17] It was later discovered that he had been suffering from mental illness.

▶ Education and Technology

During that same decade, the state's university systems added health science centers, maritime centers, and veterinary and law schools. The state system had over twenty four-year colleges and universities, many two-year colleges, and an institute for the deaf. There are also many private colleges, universities, and junior colleges. Today, the state also has large medical complexes and schools, some funded by private endowment such as the M. D. Anderson Medical Cancer Center in Houston.

Technology industries—communications, aircraft, and electronics—have flourished in recent years. High-tech workers were drawn to Houston by the Manned Spacecraft Center. Austin became a headquarters for computer-oriented industries, such as Dell Computer Corporation, as well as other software companies.

Today, most Texans live in cities, although there are still great areas of far West Texas that are sparsely populated. Minorities—primarily women, African Americans, and Hispanic Americans—are recognized in a way that never seemed possible fifty years ago. The days of great wealth and unlimited individual freedom are gone. Texans today know they live in a new world, and most are facing it with confidence and pride in their state.

Chapter Notes

Texas Facts

1. Mary G. Ramos, ed., *The Texas Almanac* (Dallas: Belo Corporation, 2000), pp. 5, 9, 10, 11.

Chapter 1. The State of Texas

1. Mary G. Ramos, ed., *The Texas Almanac* (Dallas: Belo Corporation, 2000), p. 5; Archie McDonald, personal correspondence with author.

2. Rupert N. Richardson, et. al., *Texas: The Lone Star State,* Eighth ed. (Upper Saddle River, N.J.: Prentice Hall, 2001), p. 3.

3. Roy R. Barkley and Mark F. Odintz, eds., *The Portable Handbook of Texas* (Austin: Texas State Historical Association, 2000), p. 557.

4. Ibid., p. 167.

Chapter 2. Land and Climate

1. Mary G. Ramos, ed., *The Texas Almanac* (Dallas: Belo Corporation, 2000), p. 57.

2. Rupert N. Richardson, et. al., *Texas: The Lone Star State,* Eighth ed. (Upper Saddle River, N.J.: Prentice Hall, 2001), pp. 3–5.

3. Ibid., p. 8.

4. Ibid.

5. Ramos, p. 5.

6. "North Central Texas Annual Weather Review: 1980's," *National Weather Service Southern Region: Dallas/Fort Worth,* n.d., <http://www.srh.noaa.gov/fwd/climo/annreview/1980s.html> (June 5, 2001).

7. Roy R. Barkley and Mark F. Odintz, eds., *The Portable Handbook of Texas* (Austin: Texas State Historical Association, 2000), p. 886.

Chapter 3. Economy

1. Mary G. Ramos, ed., *The Texas Almanac* (Dallas: Belo Corporation, 2000), pp. 577–578.

2. T. R. Fehrenbach, *Seven Keys to Texas* (El Paso: The University of Texas at El Paso, 1983), p. 47.

3. Ibid., p. 67.

4. David G. McComb, *Texas: A Modern History* (Austin: University of Texas Press, 1989), p. 173.

Chapter 4. Government

1. Roy R. Barkley and Mark F. Odintz, eds., *The Portable Handbook of Texas* (Austin: Texas State Historical Association, 2000), p. 389.

2. Rupert N. Richardson, et. al., *Texas: The Lone Star State*, eighth ed. (Upper Saddle River, N.J.: Prentice Hall, 2001), p. 437.

3. Eugene W. Jones, et. al., *Practicing Texas Politics,* seventh ed. (Boston: Houghton Mifflin, 1989), p. 52.

4. Richardson, p. 426.

5. Mary G. Ramos, ed., *The Texas Almanac* (Dallas: Belo Corporation, 2000), p. 418; Richardson, p. 445.

Chapter 5. History

1. Archie McDonald and Ben Procter, eds., *The Texas Heritage* (St. Louis, Mo.: The Forum Press, 1980), p. 14.

2. Ibid., pp. 24–25.

3. Archie McDonald, *Texas: All Hail the Mighty State* (Austin: Eakin Press, 1983), pp. 47–48; McComb, p. 36.

4. David G. McComb, *Texas: A Modern History* (Austin: University of Texas Press, 1989), p. 173.

5. Rupert N. Richardson, et. al., *Texas: The Lone Star State*, Eighth ed. (Upper Saddle River, N.J.: Prentice Hall, 2001), p. 78.

6. McDonald, *Texas: All Hail...*, p. 32.

7. McDonald, *Texas Heritage,* p. 49; *Texas: All Hail...,* pp. 82–84.

8. McDonald, *Texas Heritage,* p. 15.

9. Ibid., p. 54.

10. Ibid., p. 63.

11. Ibid., p. 112.

12. McComb, p. 74.

13. McDonald, *Texas Heritage,* p. 98.

14. McComb, p. 78.

15. Ibid., p. 121.

16. Richardson, pp. 417–418.

17. McComb, p. 173.

Further Reading

Barkley, Roy R. and Mark F. Odintz, eds. *The Portable Handbook of Texas*. Austin: Texas State Historical Association, 2000.

Bruun, Erik. *Texas*. New York: Black Dog & Leventhal Publishers, Inc., 2001.

Hennech, Michael C. *Texas History According to Us*. Alto, N.Mex.: Ale Publishing Company, 1991.

Marsh, Carole. *Texas History!: Surprising Secrets about Our State's Founding Mothers, Fathers, & Kids!* Peachtree City, Ga.: Gallopade International, 1996.

————. *Texas Timeline: A Chronology of Texas History, Mystery, Trivia, Legend, Lore & More*. Peachtree City, Ga.: Gallopade International, 1994.

McComb, David G. *Texas: A Modern History*. Austin: University of Texas Press, 1989.

————. *Texas: An Illustrated History*. New York: Oxford University Press, 1995.

Ramos, Mary, ed. *The Texas Almanac: 2000*. Dallas: Belo Corporation, 2000.

Richardson, Rupert N., et. al. *Texas: The Lone Star State*, eighth ed. Upper Saddle River, N.J.: Prentice Hall, 2001.

Sanford, William R. *The Chisholm Trail in American History*. Berkeley Heights, N.J.: Enslow Publishers, Inc., 2000.

Weems, John E. *The Story of Texas*. Fredericksburg, Tex.: Shearer Publishing, 1992.

Back   Forward   Stop   Review   Home   Explore   Favorites   History

Index